The Beautiful Gift

ROBBIE CLASBY

Michael Terence
Publishing

For my BELOVED MOTHER
for her never-ending belief in me.

For My BELOVED LIFE PARTNER, MICHAEL

My BESTIE,
JAN JONES

My COPY TYPIST,
AMANDA WEAKFORD

And my PUBLISHERS,
MICHAEL TERENCE PUBLISHING,
who took me on at first go.

The Beautiful Gift

Well, I'm really going, after all this time. I'm off to Marsay.

Where's that?

Out of England. Abroad. It's in French France.

Why you goin' there?

Because I can, because it's there, because I want to. I've saved hard for ages. I've got ever such a lot of trains to get on. Hope I don't get lost.

Where are the travel brochures? I asked.

What do I want them for?

I'll see it when I get there, won't I?

But you don't know where you will stay.

I'll find out, won't I?

Where will you start from?

I'm going to Gatwick by taxi, then on an aeroplane, then buses and that.

You can't go alone, you're only 17.

I'm not on my own, I've got some other passengers goin' too.

But you won't know anybody.

I will, though. I'll get the bus drivers to tell me where I can stay.

Seems a bit chancy to me.

Oh please let me go. I've wanted this for so long now and I read this book from the lending library and it's lovely there.

You don't know the language.

I'll get a phrase book with pictures.

No, you don't understand, you can't just arrive and stay with no plans.

But I'll find someone who will tell me. Don't spoil it all for me. Someone will know.

You're being daft, daft as a brush.

Look, I'll go to a travel shop and ask them.

Can I come with you?

What! To Marsay?

No, the travel people.

***

In the end, I gave in. It wasn't easy, but her heart was set on things.

The travel shop showed us some hostels for people on their own; backpackers and such.

Finally, it was agreed she'd be getting her taxi to Gatwick, as she'd wanted, then a long wait for her plane to be called.

When she arrived, she'd be guided on the rest of the journey.

***

The places to stay turned out to be expensive and hard to find, but a local taxi driver knew a friend of a friend who would oblige. Somebody's sister who owned a pub and had a few spare rooms she needed filling.

Finally, exhausted, she was shown a very tiny but clean room. The door had a lock, but she'd push something up close to make sure she was safe.

The landlady made her hot chocolate. It was a bit on the strong side, with not enough sugar, but it was very welcome.

She unpacked. It was dark outside, but her bed was clean, fresh and beautifully made up. She would inspect at leisure when she woke in the morning.

She lay there, feeling grown up and in control of her life.

***

The noise of the early morning dust carts awoke her. Rubbing her eyes, she got up and pulled the heavy drapes open and was delighted with the pretty view of a waterway.

She had her own bath, her very own bath!

Some lavender toilet things were in a little basket, fluffy towel, mauve, which matched the soaps, a beautiful jug and basin were on an old dresser, pretty, old, but not posh.

She brushed her hair, dropped the brush, which went scuttling under the bed.

A blue and white pot! What's that doing hidden away for? It was obviously part of the jug and bowl set. Navy and white, but more ornate.

Why would you put such a lovely thing under the bed where nobody could see it?

She reminded herself she wasn't in England but French France, and they must do things differently.

The clock outside the window told her it was still only early, 6 A.M.

She opened a packet of Woodbines, shook one out.

She shouldn't start, but feeling grown up and nobody to stop her, why not?

She struck a match, lit, inhaled, and nearly choked.

It wasn't very nice at all, but she'd persevere and show sophistication that right there and then she didn't feel.

She used the bath, refilled it twice as the water chilled laying in the hot soapy water. Oh, this is the life. I'm Lady Muck now!

Later, venturing down the stairs, she found a welcoming fire in the grate with extra wood nearby and a copper coal scuttle.

The landlady asked if she cared to eat. She hadn't thought of food in her excitement.

Did you sleep well, madam?

Who was she talking to? She looked behind her, but then understood it was herself being asked!

Madam.

It sounded so posh.

She was offered strong black coffee. It was bitter and she wrinkled her nose, not having tasted anything like it before.

She was used to milky tea with plenty of sugar, and toast that she'd always had to scrape.

Tiny pastry things arrived, hot, delicious, full of butter. No porridge here! A tiny wedge of creamy cheese she was told was Brie.

Having no idea what she would find outside, she asked if there were any shops that sold pretty things to take home.

After much explaining in broken English, she was directed to the markets.

The stall holders were smiley and one was free to pick things up and look around.

She found a square block of soap with a round disk on top. It smelled lovely, like Sunlight only more fancy. Evening in Paris perfume in a tiny navy blue bottle, lace, ribbons, bobbins, all sorts of wonderful things she's never really been interested in before.

Perfumed candles, pot pourri, tiny lavender bags, beaded purses, pretty jewellery made of pasta but mirror-backed to make it sparkle.

Foreign tongues called out the fish, meat and cheese stalls.

All very beautiful, all very different, fresh vegetables, not only carrots and spuds, but asparagus, courgettes and loads of fruit.

She could've spent all day just wandering around, so much to see and do.

She found pottery and glass dishes, vases, ornaments, but nothing so pretty as the bowl under her bed.

She saw bouquet hotels, and thought that's what they were called, and dogs being walked of all sizes. Some small and fluffy being carried, some too big to tuck neatly under an arm and fed titbits to.

Lots of cats, very thin, hungry, not like the cats at home who sat by the fire licking their paws and washing behind their tiny pointed ears.

Shoes, dresses, pretty things inviting touch and admiration, but nothing she particularly took a yearning to.

High-heeled slippers with fur, beautiful large coloured scarves big enough to cover her bed.

It was lovely to see the town, though, but so different to what she had at home.

She must write, but where would she get a postcard and stamp?

What would she write?

Lovely here, wish you were with me.

But she didn't want anyone with her! This was her 'Grown Up Adventure' she was sure was one of a kind rather than the first of many.

If you went back to the same place again, it wouldn't be the same as she'd found it. So many things changed and she would be that much older.

She'd found her phrase book unhelpful, the words strange and unpronounceable, and pointed to the pictures instead, pleasing herself with the fact that she'd been, seen and done so much. She'd come as a girl but promised herself to return a woman of the world. (She had much to learn, but that is the naivety of youth.)

Soon, she had to return to the pub and its smoky smell of beer, fine ales, wines, and that beautiful fireplace and comfy padded chairs.

The landlady welcomed her back and tried to converse with her about the brother of hers and the cab driver and what had she thought of her day's ventures.

She showed her what she had bought in the market place. Not a great deal, but choice things that had taken her eye.

She bought the pretty postcards, written them, put strange stamps on each, and her new friend posted them for her, saying they wouldn't possibly arrive before herself got home.

No matter.

A postcard from French France, how good was that!

She had arrived, done what she'd set out to do and come home to tell the tale.

If she never never went away again, it wouldn't matter. She was here now and so excited.

The evening dinner was something called Beef Bourguignon, tiny cut up cubes of meat, whole baby mushrooms and onions, real red wine and delicious. Afterwards came tarte tatin – apple tart, all beautifully layered out, covered in a sweet sticky glaze, such taste that she thought it food of the Gods.

She was offered a stone hot water bottle to ward off the chill. It was so heavy, but stayed hot all night long and was still warm in the morning.

Thicky foggy rain had descended overnight, so she didn't venture out at all.

She went downstairs with her book, a journal – she must, must, must record every tiny detail of what she'd seen, heard, done.

A man came round giving roses to each lady visitor. How romantic, wonderful these French France people could be, a tiny red rosebud.

She had never ever had that before in her life.

After a few days in the lovely pot she had pressed it flat in her journal to take home, pristine, timeless as the day itself.

Time was going so fast, faster than she'd ever imagined it could. She pondered about what else to amuse herself. The choice was plenty.

Waterways to look at were enchanting, but water as a way of getting from one place to another was daunting. She hadn't really liked paddling as a child but had sat on the sand watching others.

She'd seen advertised at the dock a boat trip to one of the local 'must see places'.

She took a deep breath and bought her ticket hoping it would stay calm.

The skipper had said she would be fine and there would be others to talk to.

He spoke of the cats at home, telling her that whatever he caught was for them. Being an animal lover, she hoped to catch something they could share and enjoy.

He'd done as promised and baited her hooks for her. The thought of touching that live bait made her queasy. He was charming and friendly, reminding her of her favourite uncle she'd had as a kid.

Back at the pub, it was warm and inviting, but as always very smoky. The fire smoked back into the room at odd times, the men with pipes and cigars, the cigarettes had a camel on the packet, and the ashtrays were always full.

She tasted red wine for the first time ever and it was dry as vinegar. It hadn't tasted like that in the stew, but on its own it was bitter.

People sang and a lot of the women she noticed were dressed in a theatrical way; low tops, overly-painted faces like actresses, and very popular with the gents, who bought them many drinks and laughed loudly.

She retired to her own room and read her journal, pleased that she'd actually been allowed to come.

She found on her bed an extra warm blanket and a huge orange cat that purred its head off and she told him he was beautiful.

I'd call you Marmaduke if you were mine. Huge green eyes gazed at her, as it had done many, many times before to other guests who had been delighted to find him.

If you visit me after my boat trip, I might have some titbits for you, she told him as she scratched his fluffy ears.

He blinked at her slowly as if he understood what she was telling him.

We've got cats at home. They sleep in the barns with the horses, all warm and content, sleeping cat dreams.

He was still there when she woke, but when she left the bed he didn't stir.

***

Morning came with heavy rain and was cold, but it didn't last.

She had breakfast as before of delicious pastries, fresh fruits, juice, and bitter coffee which was changed for hot chocolate.

She dressed warmly, but as the day grew it got very warm and the boat trip was a delight.

She was lucky with her catch. The skipper was pleased and no doubt his cats, too.

What the fish were called she had no idea, but they shimmered beautifully and were a decent size not to be thrown back in the water.

She tasted sea urchins, tiny salted creatures that looked like a conker in its brown shell, brown bread made locally and plenty of sour tasting wine that she didn't care for but was too polite to refuse.

Some people decided to dive off the boat, but not being a swimmer let them get on with it.

The skipper said again about his cats and a very poorly sister at home. They were close and said he'd been a fisherman since boyhood, having had the boat handed down through many generations.

She didn't catch his name. It was something very foreign that she would forget anyway.

As the boat gently rocked, her eyes grew heavy and gave in to sleep.

She woke to notice her arms had pinkened by the sun, but her sleep hadn't caused her to miss anything.

As she left the boat, the skipper, unseen by other passengers, handed her the most beautiful shell. It had a pearl lustre and fitted the palm of her hand. He wrapped her fingers around it and told her it was his gift from the sea.

She put it in her bag and promised herself she'd treasure it forever.

The orange cat meowed as she returned and was rewarded with one of the sea urchins. He tucked into his treat, yawned, purred, and folded himself back to sleep on her pillows.

The landlady appeared with a tray full of tiny cakes, brioche and hot drink, saying that it would be too noisy downstairs for a young lady on her own. The men had been gambling and lost huge amounts of money and were a little too disruptive.

Her bed and orange cat were the only company needed to drift into a deep and dreamless sleep.

The sea air had made her sleepy, sleepier than she'd ever thought possible.

She'd always been told that if you put a shell to your ear, you hear the sea where that very shell came from. Was it a myth? A romantic old wives' tale? She had no way of knowing, but she heard the sea loud and clear and smiled at the memories of the kind man who'd given it to her.

***

Breakfast was welcome. She was so hungry and relished what was on her plate this morning, as it turned out it was delicious fluffy scrambled eggs, no doubt from the landlady's own batch of hens, tiny pieces of toast, lashings of the finest French salted butter, and as she'd mentioned a pot of tea, sadly Earl Grey, which she wasn't used to and couldn't take a taste to.

The landlady had quite taken to her ladylike English ways and passed a happy chat with her while business had a lull. She liked the girl and hoped to see her return someday. Her sons were trawlermen, but she didn't see them much these days, so being with female company was pleasant.

She hoped the postcards would arrive for the loved ones before the girl arrived home. All the stamps had been first class and gone out with the first mail boat, but the English Channel was a long strip of water to cross.

She counted her remaining money and was very pleased to find she hadn't dug deeply into what was in her purse so far.

She would leave flowers as a gift when she left, and was not in too much of a hurry to leave.

She missed home – the stables, the horses, cats, her real life, but her adventure into adulthood was equally more than she'd dreamed of.

She held the shell to her ear and admired the lovely pot under her bed, knowing there was a very welcome place awaiting them at home.

She told herself that this was her destiny, something she had to do for herself, and was proud she'd followed it through, but it had been and was still very daunting and new.

There were no phones at home and she could have only got through by asking somebody to be in a phone box at a given time, times being different here, but she'd written and told them she was safe and not to worry.

She felt she had already come such a long way, not just her journey but self-discovery, too. She could survive, she'd proven it, done so many things that she would have deemed out of her world, met people who she would not have known.

The markets, the boat trip, being on her own to make her own decisions, choices.

She'd not failed in supporting herself, not been pickpocketed, they wouldn't dare!

She was her own woman and at 17 was doing better than anybody, better than she herself had ever expected. She could've turned tail and gone home!

Today was the start of the rest of her life and she was in charge!

She might not know the language, but so much was expression and gesture anyway, and using her phrasebook pictures at least she never went hungry.

The food was amazing, wherever she went, so refined, so dainty, so delicious.

She could order a drink too if the fancy took her.

A lot had been down to plain common sense; avoiding crowds, back streets, and those who try to sell what you don't want.

She had a couple of books to read anyway and her landlady had available, not that she asked much of her.

The Woodbines had died a death. She had tried to smoke them as adults do but they were ghastly and made her feel quite unwell.

The coffee was unpalatable as well, the hot chocolate needed more sugar, but those tiny cakes and pastries were her downfall and she loved them.

Street markets did lovely pralines, hot chestnuts and chocolates worthy of buying to take home.

She'd enjoyed watching the elderly ladies, with their trolleys full of newspaper, feeding the wild cats, and later seeing them all empty, and the cats sitting on the benches next day in the sun shone with full extended bellies.

The sound of early dustcarts when she was still tucked up in her cosy, warm bed, more so if it was raining hard outside.

The singing downstairs in the early hours, the smells, the sounds, there was just nothing to compare.

But today she was making her list of what to take back for whom. Oh those pastries her landlady provided and tiny cakes, square, full of alcohol and covered in green icing; the meringues covered in pink chocolate on lollypop sticks, the cheeses!

Today she'd go back to the markets and look at stalls she had missed before.

Pretty glass dressing table sets, table runners, hair combs of tortoise shell, toiletries, lavender, rosebud balls, spices, jams, and even fripperies, perfumed stationery for loved ones, more pretty picture postcards.

She may even return to the fishing port, the crab and lobster were treats to behold and she would never have that at home.

The saved money had gone far indeed, with still plenty left. Maybe she'd buy a picture for her wall if she found what she fancied, a handheld mirror. No good sitting thinking, she'd go out this very minute and look.

She enjoyed a croque monsieur in a café – cheese and bacon toasted sandwich that melted in the mouth and made her want another. Delicious chips called frites, and all types of garlic sauces to add to them.

She'd head back to the jetty to see what was going on. Maybe another boat trip or ride on a horse through town.

When she ran out of inspiration, she would seek ideas from her landlady, who was kind, motherly and helpful without being overbearing.

She returned to the pottery and lace-making works.

She passed beggars asking for centimes – she had a pocketful and they were heavy. She knew they would value them, but couldn't give to all. She chose the sick, ill, thin that nobody else bothered with, but there were so many.

Feeling the weight of the things she'd bought at the market, she went back to the pub.

Some sort of stew was cooking, thought she could smell fish, but wasn't really sure that fish was stewed. The landlady said it was bouillabaisse and made of seafood. She was fond of shellfish and was offered a bowl to warm her up.

Well, fish and chips were always looked forward to, but this was something completely new. It was strongly flavoured with a lot of garlic, tasty enough but she didn't want more of it.

She mopped up the liquid with her bread, but put the fish bits in a napkin to give Orange Cat later.

He was nowhere to be seen.

***

She went back upstairs. He was on her bed. His eyes opened lazily, then she opened the napkin and he smelled what she had brought in for him. The huge green eyes blinked in rapture, the pink tongue licking his lips. He washed, then went back to his dreams on her pillow, kneading it and making it comfy.

A few evenings passed before she noticed it on the menu again. It was obviously a very popular dish, but one that didn't appeal.

She wrote in her journal, read a couple of chapters of her book, indulged in her hot bath with toiletries she'd found left on her bed – rose, very strong and sweet. It was oil and didn't bubble up, but made the water and her skin velvet soft.

She had large pink fluffy towels, beautifully folded and scented like the bath oil.

Drifting off to sleep, she made a mental note to buy pencils and colours and draw in her journal some of the scenery, if she could master it.

Definitely she would try to draw Orange Cat, but she'd do it lightly at first, smudging hard lines with her fingertip to give the impression of things she couldn't draw.

She'd go down to the bench by the waterway and take in the atmosphere as she drew, wondering hopefully her landlady would provide a box of something she could take with her to eat at leisure.

***

She woke up in cold bath water. Two choices: refill with hot water and bury down for a while, or go to bed. She chose the bed and done with it, she didn't really want to wake again in the bath.

Wrapped up in the warm bed, she finally drifted off, dreaming of boats, lots of fish, and quayside goings on, and that big stolen crab she'd seen one of the harbour cats run off with.

The changing light as the day went by, the sounds she was enjoying but unused to.

She slept well into late morning.

***

A large velvet paw resting on her cheek woke her gently. She wondered if the cat was like this with everyone. He rubbed his head on her neck as if she were his world.

She'd overslept by a long time, but padded downstairs hoping it wasn't too late.

She put the rest of the Woodbines on a table. Somebody else would make do of them.

Conversing as much as she could with her landlady, who drew her a map, the local art shop would sell her pastiche and conte crayons, maybe a charcoal stick.

She'd asked and got her food parcel, which was neatly packed in a wicker hamper basket; delicious sandwiches, cakes, fruit and a bottle of 'presse'.

She managed to find out that her room was favoured by the cat, and although he was affectionate, he wouldn't be picked up or sit on her lap, and his wishes so far had been as they were.

Much to her delight, she found postcards exactly capturing the scenery, not photographs but what local artists had done. Then she came across the one of the orange cat, well not him but his likeness, sitting outside a blue door on a step.

She bought several, meaning to frame and put on her wall at home. She found and bought some beautiful patchwork bed covers. They cost more than she'd wanted to pay for. She shook her head and walked on. A small boy grabbed her elbow, gesturing for her to follow him back to the stall. The man lowered his hand and signalling he would drop the price. He took a pencil stub from behind his ear, licked it and wrote how much he would accept.

Smiling and nodding to each other, he wrapped the covers in brown paper, sealed it with wax and nodded in thanks again.

They were lovely, and although being not too bad herself with a needle, these were rich, expensive colours – mauves, olives, saffrons, turquoise, rich deep greens, smoky rose madder.

She found glass friendship globes made at the end of the day by girls at the glass-blowing works who kept them for gifts to give at Christmas.

She thought they would be too fragile to take home in case they broke on her journey.

She would capture them on paper and show her journal as a lasting memento to all whom cared to know.

Passing flower sellers who had baskets and baskets of lavender in all variations of whites, pinks, rose, purple hues she'd been unaware of and with tiny floaty leaf-like petals.

Obviously some other types grew here, stronger scented, more robust, enough maybe to wrap and take home.

Another stall was selling cheese, all wrapped in cream muslin with strange names and stranger aromas.

The stall holder, seeing her interest, cut several tiny pieces off and offered them on greased paper, some soft and creamy as butter, some crumbled and some very hard, ones with blue threads, others with olives, capers, red things that looked like cherries but tasted totally different.

Fresh eggs, tiny and white, grey speckled, rich dark browns, some duck eggs, large, but not as large as the goose eggs, and would probably fill a whole frying pan.

Jars of clear honey with pieces of cone inside, conserves with thick paper lids held down by rubber bands or waxed string.

Bottles of all sizes of home-made lemonade with china stoppers and wire cage.

She bought one, flicked the cage, unstopped the bottle and drank deeply. Not too sour, not too sweet, full of flavour, slightly scented. She stopped the lid back on and bagged it for later.

She still had her hamper, so sat quietly to eat, drink and enjoy what her generous landlady had packed for her.

***

Evening was drawing in, so she made her way back to the pub, where she quickly made ready for bed after returning the landlady's basket with many merci beaucoup as she'd learnt meant thank you.

In her pretty little wooden bed, she thought of all she had to take back with her. There seemed to be so much, nothing of which she'd bought and wished she hadn't, and really was nothing she'd wanted but didn't have the money for.

She would ask her landlady if she would be able to help her. She picked up the lovely bowl for the hundredth time and wondered if the landlady would sell it to her.

She'd explain that she'd not been able to find another, and with a little bag full of francs and centimes was hoping she'd have enough to pay. She had notes left too that hadn't been broken into. It might take some of those too.

She could visualise it full of tulips, daffodils, hyacinths, carnations, maybe a rose or two, on a small table at home. She would buy the flowers at home and present the whole thing when her mother least expected it!

***

She heard the deep familiar yowling miaow and unlocked her door.

Marmaduke walked in, tail high, huge green eyes watching her. Jumping on her bed, he purred and snuggled himself down.

She would miss him, but as pretty as he was she couldn't imagine him in any other setting. It had been the same with things she'd picked up, examined but left on the market stalls. A place for everything and everything in its place.

And their place was here in beautiful French France.

Hers was at home and she wouldn't've wanted it to be any other way.

She'd spent three glorious weeks here already, but time had flown by.

It's not the end, she reminded herself, it's the beginning of a new chapter as a travelled woman.

***

As it was, the landlady was only too glad to help this young woman. She'd packed all the things neatly into a large case of her own which had sat idly on top of a wardrobe for years. It was a trunk which had seen better days, but was gladly received.

***

The journey home was uneventful, spent sleeping, and had been taken care of by her landlady at the airport. The staff had guided her, and at Gatwick, to her delight, was the local baker's van to drive her home.

The beautiful pot?

The landlady had laughed and made a gift of it, accepting no money. The flowers she had produced were more than gratefully received.

***

On the hall table, taking pride of place on a huge white round of French France lace, stands a beautiful chamber pot full of spring flowers.

25

Available worldwide from Amazon

Michael Terence
Publishing

www.mtp.agency

mtp.agency

@mtp_agency